The Child-Seeking Heart: Waiting and the Miracle

Credendo vides — Believe, and you will see

Dildora Ibrohimova

Ukiyoto Publishing

All global publishing rights are held by

Ukiyoto Publishing

Published in 2025

Content Copyright © Dildora Ibrohimova

ISBN 9789370095670

All rights reserved.

No part of this publication may be reproduced, transmitted, or stored in a retrieval system, in any form by any means, electronic, mechanical, photocopying, recording or otherwise, without the prior permission of the publisher.

The moral rights of the author have been asserted.

This book is sold subject to the condition that it shall not by way of trade or otherwise, be lent, resold, hired out or otherwise circulated, without the publisher's prior consent, in any form of binding or cover other than that in which it is published.

www.ukiyoto.com

This book is dedicated to all those who never lost hope and keep believing in miracles.

Acknowledgement

I sincerely thank my family, friends, and all the people who supported me on this journey. Your love and encouragement made this book possible.

Author's Note – I Have Walked This Path Too

In the name of Allah, the Most Gracious, the Most Merciful.

Infertility and secondary infertility have sadly become increasingly common challenges in today's world. This is not merely a medical condition, but a deeply personal struggle — one that affects marriages, emotions, and even the soul. In response, many clinics and IVF centers have emerged to offer modern solutions.

IVF is often seen as the final hope. But despite all scientific advances, it cannot guarantee success — because the ultimate outcome lies with Allah's will. Yet for families living through the pain of childlessness, faith alone sometimes feels difficult to hold onto. They seek hope in medicine, in doctors, in procedures.

I know this pain firsthand. I lived in that waiting — for ten long years. Month after month, I hoped, I prayed, I watched the calendar with trembling hands — only to end in tears again and again. I was one of those women who cried in the silence of night, who smiled for others but was breaking inside. Every time someone joyfully announced their pregnancy, my heart would quietly bleed. Only someone who has endured it truly understands this sorrow.

It was this journey, these feelings, that led me to write this book. Because sometimes, the most comforting voice isn't the expert's — it's the one who has been there too. I want to offer you something deeper than advice: comfort, courage, and companionship. I know this pain is not only physical — it's spiritual. It can shake your identity, your marriage, your prayers.

My sincere hope is that this book will be more than just pages to read — I want it to become a companion to your heart. May it bring you light, patience, and strength. Because after every storm, skies clear. After every night, dawn arrives. So never lose hope. Allah's mercy is endless, and His power has no limits. You, too, will find your joy — inshaAllah. Just believe, act, and turn your waiting into a form of worship.

In these pages, I'll share with you what helped me: the mindset, the prayers, the emotional tools, and the faith that carried me through. Try them if you wish — maybe, just maybe, Allah will fill your arms with the miracle you long for. InshaAllah.

Contents

A Story of Hope — 1

"Mercy Surpasses Power" — 1

Comfort — You Are Not Alone — 3

Rule One — 5

No Illness Is Without a Cure — 5

Rule Two: Be Steadfast in Worship — 9

Rule Three: The Answer Hidden in the Subconscious — 12

Rule Four: Transform Your State — Transform Your Fate — 16

Rule 5: Restoring Feminine and Masculine Energy — 20

Rule Six: Listen to Your Inner Voice — It Always Knows the Way — 26

Rule Seven: The Door of Charity and Generosity — 31

Epilogue — 35

About the Author — *41*

A Story of Hope
"Mercy Surpasses Power"

(An Ancient Tale)

A woman once came to the Prophet of Allah, Musa (peace be upon him), with a heartfelt plea:

"O Prophet of Allah, please pray to your Lord for me," she said. "Let Him bless me with a righteous child who will fill my heart with joy."

Musa (peace be upon him) made the supplication. But Allah responded:

"I have written her as 'aqeem' — barren."

When Musa (peace be upon him) conveyed this response, the woman lowered her head and walked away in silence.

A year passed. She returned once again, her eyes full of hope.

"O Prophet of Allah, please pray once more. Perhaps my Lord will grant me a gift."

Musa (peace be upon him) prayed again. And once again, Allah responded:

"She is aqeem. It is written in her destiny."

Time passed. Days turned into months. One day, Musa (peace be upon him) saw that same woman — holding a baby in her arms.

2 The Child-Seeking Heart: Waiting and the Miracle

"Whose child is this?" he asked in astonishment.

"He is my son," she replied, her face glowing with joy.

Bewildered, Musa (peace be upon him) turned to his Lord and asked:

"O my Lord, did You not declare her barren? How then does she now have a child?"

Allah the Most Merciful answered:

"Yes, every time I declared her barren, she called Me 'Ar-Raheem' — The Most Merciful.

So My mercy overcame My decree."

Moral: Even when destiny seems sealed, Allah's mercy knows no bounds.

Patience and unwavering faith are the keys to miracles.

The heart that trusts may not know when its prayer will be answered,

but it continues to live in hope — and that hope is, in itself, a prayer.

Comfort — You Are Not Alone

According to a report by the World Health Organization (WHO), approximately 17.5% of the global adult population—one in every six people—struggles with infertility. The report highlights that infertility is a major public health issue across all countries and regions, regardless of income level.

"The most important takeaway from this report is that infertility does not discriminate. It affects people from every background and every income level," said WHO Director-General Dr.Tedros Adhanom Ghebreyesus. "The large number of people affected shows the urgent need to expand access to fertility care and make sure that infertility is no longer overlooked. Every person who wishes to become a parent should have the support they need — through safe, effective, and affordable medical options."

Despite the scope of the issue, access to prevention, diagnosis, and treatment — including assisted reproductive technologies like in vitro fertilization (IVF) — remains limited and expensive. Many people are left without access to care simply because they cannot afford it.

Pascal Allotey, WHO's Director for Sexual and Reproductive Health and Research, noted that millions of people face devastating medical costs when seeking treatment for infertility, often pushing them into poverty. This financial burden has become one of the key factors driving health inequality around the world.

While this latest report provides reliable global evidence on the prevalence of infertility, it also notes a serious lack of systematic data in many countries and regions. WHO is calling for stronger national efforts to collect infertility statistics in order to better understand who is affected, improve treatment access, and develop strategies to reduce infertility risks.

The report is based on over 100 studies conducted between 1990 and 2021. (Originally published on April 4, 2023, by Qalampir.uz)

Sharing this data is meant to offer you comfort — to remind you that you are not alone. You are not the only one carrying this weight. Around the world, many hearts are walking this same path. Many of them understand your pain, your silence, and your questions.

I know some trials are so deep and personal that only those who have walked through them truly understand. And as someone who lived through this struggle for ten years, I tell you this: every night has its dawn. Every storm has its end. And every season of patience bears fruit, in time.

Rule One
No Illness Is Without a Cure

I truly believe that there is no illness in this world without a cure. Even for something as common and seemingly minor as the flu, healing only happens by the will and permission of God. We often assume that medicine or antibiotics are the main cure, but they are only tools. True healing comes through the power of the Creator.

The flu has become so ordinary and familiar to us that we treat it as just another seasonal discomfort. Pharmacies offer various remedies, and we take them with confidence. It's often this very confidence that speeds up our recovery.

Infertility, in reality, is a condition just like any other. But unlike the flu, we've surrounded it with heavy emotional burdens and deep psychological grief, which makes it harder to accept as a natural part of life. Imagine if there were a guaranteed treatment for infertility — and if we accepted it with the same trust and lightness as we do flu medicine — perhaps we'd see recovery much faster.

That's why the first step must be to break down the mental walls we've built around infertility. We must learn to approach it naturally, seeing it not as a punishment, but as a test — and even an opportunity

— from God. This shift in perspective can change your inner state. It awakens hope, and it revives trust.

Remember: every healing begins with belief. When hope, trust, and surrender to God are present in your heart, your efforts are empowered by His mercy. So don't focus on the pain — focus on the healing. Don't wait for hardship — expect divine assistance. And know that His will is greater than anything.

Credendo vides ~ Believe, and you will see.

Your belief is one of the most powerful tools you have in overcoming infertility. I love a Latin phrase that beautifully expresses this truth: credendo vides — "by believing, you will see."

Human nature often wants to see before it believes. But real transformation, and deep spiritual growth, begins in the opposite direction. First, believe. Then, the evidence will appear in your life.

Every great idea, every inner healing, every dream — begins with belief. Before your eyes can see, your heart must believe. That's when life begins to open its secrets.

To believe means to believe in yourself, to trust in God's plan, to have faith in healing, and to hold firm to the possibility of goodness.

So if you desire change, begin by believing.

And as I reminded you in the story of the woman once declared barren — her destiny was rewritten by faith. That story is your invitation to discover the power of belief.

Reflection Questions

1. Do you truly believe healing is possible for you?

If not, what inner block might be preventing that belief?

2. Have you ever experienced a time when belief led to unexpected positive results?

What can that experience teach you now?

3. How does your faith in God influence your healing journey?

Do you allow room for His will to work through your efforts?

4. What small step can you take today to shift from focusing on pain to focusing on healing?

🌿 Summary Insight

Belief is not a passive feeling — it is an active force that invites healing into your life. When you choose to believe in God's mercy, in your own resilience, and in the hidden wisdom of your situation, you begin to open the doors to transformation. Let your heart lead the way with faith, and let your belief become the foundation of your journey.

Rule Two: Be Steadfast in Worship

No matter what faith you belong to, overcoming this trial begins with steadfastness in worship. Worship is a direct connection between a human being and the Creator. It lightens the burden of sorrow in the heart — where your strength ends, His power begins.

As a follower of Islam, I want to share that in the darkest and most hopeless times of my life, what brought me ease was returning to prayer. I had learned to perform the five daily prayers during my university years, but as time passed, I drifted away due to life's distractions and my own laziness. Then one day, God gave me a heavy but deeply honorable trial — infertility. Through this test, I turned back to Him.

In that moment, I realized I wasn't just facing a hardship — I was being drawn into a greater purpose tied to His mercy. When all other doors seemed closed, He opened the door of worship to me. And through that door came peace to my soul, comfort to my heart, and hope to my life.

Worship is not only about prostration — it's about filling the heart with faith, surrendering your wishes with good expectations, and living with hope. Worship feeds the soul. It saves you from falling apart and frees you from the question: "Am I worthy?" Because to be worthy of God's mercy, you don't need to be perfect — His mercy is given freely and without limits.

Reflection Questions

1. How does steadfast worship help in overcoming difficult trials in life?

2. In what ways can worship bring peace and hope to a troubled heart?

3. Have you experienced a moment when returning to faith or worship helped you through a challenging time? How did it change your perspective?

4. What does it mean to surrender your wishes with good expectations in the context of worship?

Summary

Steadfastness in worship is a powerful anchor during life's hardest trials. It connects us directly to the Creator, lightening the weight of sorrow and filling our hearts with peace and hope. Worship is not only a ritual but a deep spiritual surrender, a way to trust in mercy beyond perfection. Through steadfast prayer and faith, we find strength beyond our own limits and open ourselves to a greater purpose and comfort even in the darkest times

Rule Three: The Answer Hidden in the Subconscious

Pay special attention to this rule. For me, this realization was the key to the puzzle — and perhaps it will be for you too. But for this key to work in your life, the previous rules must become your way of life.

One night, I cried endlessly. Bowing down before God in deep agony over my infertility, I poured out my heart in prayer:

"Oh my Creator! If You intend to bless me with a child, then give them to me. But if You have decreed to withhold this gift from me, then call me back to You, so all this torment may end!"

These weren't just pleas — they were an act of true surrender.

A week later, I began to feel a strange pull toward a bookstore called "Kitoblar olami" ("World of Books") in the city of Bukhara. I didn't know why I felt drawn there or what I was meant to do once inside. This store is one of the largest book hypermarkets in the city. Somehow, I found myself wandering through the aisles until I ended up in the psychology section. I picked up about ten books and sat down at the reading desk. I opened each book at random and began reading.

Four of them spoke to me deeply, and I decided to buy them. Among them were "Love Your Disease" and "Vaccinate Yourself Against Stress" by Valery Sinelnikov, "The Magic" by Rhonda Byrne, and "The Four Steps to Happiness" by Joe Vitale.

Although I was working in an editorial office at the time, I spent most of my free hours reading these psychological books and trying to apply their teachings in my life. Through Sinelnikov's book "Love Your Disease" — which I highly recommend — I began to learn how to speak with my subconscious.

According to Sinelnikov, infertility often stems from unresolved childhood trauma or subconscious programming. He suggests that many infertile individuals received the message "a child is not needed" in some form during childhood. When I read that, I began to dig into my own past. One childhood memory came vividly to mind: during an argument, my father once shouted at me in anger, "It would be better if you didn't exist!" I hadn't understood the full meaning of those words as a child, but they had deeply imprinted themselves in my heart.

That moment had programmed my subconscious with the belief: "My existence has no value." And for years, I had been living according to that script. When I realized that this belief could be one of the reasons I was being denied the gift of motherhood, something inside me stirred. It was time for change — time to rewrite my internal programming.

It wasn't easy, but it was possible. Sinelnikov outlines step-by-step how to do this. With his guidance, I began to plant new seeds of mercy, love, and self-acceptance in my subconscious. I learned to forgive myself. I learned to love myself. And I learned to see myself as someone worthy of becoming a mother.

Remember: Some illnesses don't require healing of the body — they require healing of the subconscious.

It's not just the heart that must believe — the mind must also become open to belief.

Reflect on these questions:

What are my deepest, most hidden beliefs about myself? Do they serve me or hinder me?

Do I truly believe I am worthy of having a child? If not, when and where did that belief begin?

Am I in communication with my Creator? Do I feel His will and love in my life?

Am I ready to change the subconscious patterns that are blocking me?

Summary

Cleansing the subconscious and reprogramming internal beliefs is a crucial step in the journey to overcoming infertility. It means identifying the harmful beliefs you hold about yourself and replacing them with thoughts that bring healing and hope.

Never forget: True healing begins in the mind — and only then does it manifest in the body.

There was a time I believed I didn't deserve to be a mother. I was irritable, anxious, unable to fully express love — and I saw my infertility as punishment. But that thinking is the seed of hopelessness planted by Satan. Because God is forgiving, loving, and merciful. He has better plans for you than even you have for yourself.

So, if you want to stand strong against your trials, strengthen your worship. This is the first key to trust. Through faith and prayer, we tie our incomplete strength to the power of the Creator. And that connection — it's the key that opens the door to miracles.

Remember: Worship is your door to speak with your Creator — and that door is never closed.

Rule Four: Transform Your State — Transform Your Fate

If you truly long for a deep transformation in your life, begin by transforming yourself. Even the simplest and smallest shifts can become turning points that lead to monumental change. My heartfelt advice: start working on yourself. Consider what you can change in your external world. Rearrange your furniture. Adjust your eating habits. Pay attention to your physical body. Perhaps a change in your workplace, your communication style, your hairstyle, or even your clothing can bring a breath of fresh air to your soul.

What matters most is this: if you earnestly pursue inner change, it will inevitably guide you toward the miracles you seek.

God promises this in the Holy Qur'an:

"Indeed, Allah will not change the condition of a people until they change what is within themselves."

(Surah Ar-Ra'd, 13:11)

This verse is also a key for us on the journey of healing from infertility.

Many of us, often since childhood, have internalized certain roles — the victim, the aggressor. I had done the same. At one time, I was merciless — not just to others, but to myself. If someone upset me, I'd respond harshly. I wouldn't shy away from conflict. Then I would retreat into a lonely corner, cry, and hope someone would feel sorry for me. I took a strange comfort in playing the helpless one. Worst of all, this had become my normal.

One day, my psychologist said something that pierced my heart like an arrow:

"You've grown attached to being the victim. You want people to feel sorry for you."

That was a moment of revelation. I realized I was not only battling infertility — I was fighting against identities I had created for myself.

Reading The Magic by Rhonda Byrne, I began the daily practice of writing gratitude. At first, it felt strange, unnatural. But gradually, I felt something shifting inside me. Every line of gratitude chipped away at the darkness in my heart, allowing light to enter.

I made a conscious decision to renew my identity. I distanced myself from sorrowful music, pessimistic poetry, and films that always ended in the misfortune of the downtrodden. I worked to refresh my aura, to embrace life once more with tenderness.

And I assure you — those inner changes became the doorway to miracles in my life.

Most importantly, I learned to show mercy to myself. I gave myself love. I forgave myself.

As a Muslim woman, gratitude became a pillar of my life. No one had ever taught me to say alhamdulillah from the depths of my soul. But I discovered that for the grateful heart, Allah promises even greater blessings. Gratitude, then, is both worship and healing — the very essence of a pure heart.

Reflective Questions:

What role am I playing in my life: the oppressor, the victim, or the free soul?

Which habits am I willing to let go of?

Behind which cheerful mask am I hiding my tears?

What is keeping me from practicing gratitude?

What are the things I can give thanks for today?

Am I waiting for mercy only from others — or do I show mercy to myself?

Summary

Until a person changes themselves, life will not change. This is neither harshness nor punishment — it is a divine law woven into the fabric of existence.

The word change does not only mean action in the external world. It means internal renewal — a shift in attitude, behavior, beliefs, and emotions.

So do not be afraid of change. You are worthy of love, of blessings, of becoming a parent. All you need to do is prove your readiness — not in words, but in the way you begin to live.

Rule 5: Restoring Feminine and Masculine Energy

Part 1: Feminine Energy – The Source of Life

Conceiving a child is not only a physical process—it is also an expression of emotional, spiritual, and energetic balance. A person's relationship with their gender identity—how they feel as a man or a woman—has a direct impact on many aspects of life, including fertility.

I am a woman. That's why, in this section, I will primarily talk about feminine energy. If you are a male reader, I encourage you to skip to the second part and find what resonates with you.

Throughout my marriage, I felt myself gradually becoming more "masculine." Perhaps it was the circumstances of life, the burden of responsibility, the fight for financial stability, or simply a lack of emotional preparation. Slowly, my voice grew harsher, my mannerisms more rigid, and my heart tougher. I was so determined to protect my rights that I ended up living in a constant inner battle with my husband.

Then, one day, I realized: I am a woman—not a rival. I was not created to compete with my husband, but to lean on his shoulder and walk beside him.

Realizing this, however, wasn't enough. Restoring my feminine energy required conscious effort.

I turned to books, audio courses, and the advice of psychologists. I listened to various experts online who offered practical guidance for restoring inner grace, feminine softness, and emotional clarity. Slowly, I began to transform myself:

– Softness in my posture and movements

– Grace in my speech

– Elegance in my clothing

– Respect and trust in my relationship

At the same time, I began to identify and release the masculine protective patterns that had built up in my subconscious over the years. Because when a woman denies her femininity, her body receives a signal:

"You are a man, and men don't give birth."

These words may sound harsh, but I witnessed their truth firsthand. When a woman fails to embrace her identity—physically, emotionally, and spiritually—her nature resists the miracle of creation.

Questions to reflect on:

– Do I love my femininity, or do I resent it?

– Have I taken on the role of the protector in life? If so, why?

– What am I doing to restore my feminine essence?

– Do my clothes, posture, voice, and words reflect feminine or masculine energy?

– Do I believe I need to be strong in order to protect myself?

Through this process, I rediscovered myself. As my feminine energy began to flourish, not only did my body transform—so did my face, even my eyes. The conflicts in our marriage decreased, and we found our balance. We were no longer rivals but partners leaning on one another.

Remember: when feminine and masculine energies flow freely, life blooms naturally. But when these energies are blocked, challenges often arise—not just in personal life, but in marriage, fertility, and beyond.

Part 2: For Men — Reclaiming Inner Strength

Dear male reader, if you're reading this book in pursuit of parenthood, I respect that you're also exploring the emotional and spiritual side of the journey. Fertility is not solely a woman's concern. The true solution lies in the sacred union of two souls, two energies.

What is masculine energy?

Masculine energy is not just physical strength. It is:

– The ability to take responsibility

– The courage to make decisions

– The willingness to be a source of stability and support

– The quiet strength to protect and provide

– And above all, the power to radiate positive energy

In today's world, many men feel lost, drained, or disconnected from their sense of purpose. Emotional burdens and the pressures of life can weigh them down.

When masculine energy is depleted, several things can happen:

– A sense of instability sets in

– Nothing feels satisfying

– Constant conflict and resentment may arise with one's partner

– Even if there is a desire for a child, the subconscious may send the signal: "I'm not ready yet."

What can be done?

1. Strengthen your body and soul

Spend time in nature, practice spiritual silence, meditate or pray. Reconnect with your inner self and dignity.

2. Stop competing with your wife

She is not your opponent. She is a gift meant to support your weary spirit.

3. Connect with sources of higher energy

Prayers, sacred texts, wise mentors, and developing your "inner vision" can all elevate your awareness and balance.

4. Help your wife reconnect with her femininity

When she feels like a woman, she will empower you to feel like a man. Remember—she, too, may have lost touch with her nature. As a man, you can lead her back to it with love and strength.

Questions to reflect on:

– How do I feel as a man?

– Do I think my wife is trying to compete with me? Or have I lost my sense of leadership and presence?

– When was the last time I truly felt strong, dignified, and dependable?

Conclusion:

Man and woman—two distinct energies. When they live in harmony, not competition, a spiritual miracle occurs even before a child is conceived: peace, trust, and love. And that kind of atmosphere is the most fertile ground for new life.

Rule Six: Listen to Your Inner Voice — It Always Knows the Way

If you've ever thought to yourself, "Something inside me was trying to say something in that moment", then you've already begun to hear your inner voice.

This voice is a gentle but truthful feeling placed by God within the human heart. It often contradicts logic. Sometimes it even seems irrational. Yet its message is always unmistakably clear.

A personal story:

I hadn't been married even a few months when one of my husband's relatives asked:

— "Are you expecting a baby?"

Smiling, I replied,

— "No."

The moment that word left my mouth, two phrases flashed through my heart like lightning: "ten years" and "IVF treatment."

Where had these words come from? Why those exact phrases? I didn't reflect on it at the time. I dismissed them as meaningless thoughts, easily forgotten. But... my inner voice had already spoken.

Understanding—though it came late

Exactly ten years passed. And those two words—IVF and ten years—became a vivid part of my life's reality.

Throughout those years, I read many books. My eyes opened, my heart softened. Rhonda Byrne's "The Magic" was a turning point for me. As I practiced her 27-day gratitude challenge, I learned to treasure the small, quiet blessings of my life again. Gratitude, I discovered, is one of the most powerful pathways to divine energy.

As I explored psychological practices, I began to realize that many of the techniques recommended by modern therapists actually originated from the timeless values of Islam. This awakened a deeper sincerity within me.

Now I know: positive energy, the sacred bond of marriage, the miracle of a child — all of it begins with purity of heart and thought.

A strange question, and a subconscious block

In many psychology books, one particular question keeps showing up:

"What's the downside of becoming a parent?"

At first, I couldn't find an answer. "How could there be a downside to such a blessing?" I wondered.

But once I started working on my subconscious mind, I realized the answer had always been there — buried deep.

For years, one of my greatest dreams was to move to the United States. And hidden within my subconscious was this quiet belief:

"If I have a child, I'll lose my freedom. It will ruin my chance of moving to the U.S."

That buried thought had silently grown into a fear — the fear of motherhood as a limitation. I hadn't known that having a child could be the very path, not the obstacle.

Then one day, I reframed the idea:

"What if, through children, the way to the U.S. becomes easier? What if they are the key to my prayers?"

My mind accepted this shift with joy. The resistance in my subconscious softened, replaced by hope.

Reflection & Practice: How to Hear the Inner Voice

1. Enter stillness and contemplation

The world is full of noise, and noise drowns the inner voice.

Engage in dhikr, prayer, walks in nature, silence — all are keys to unlocking that gentle guidance.

2. Write down the words or dreams that surprise you

They may carry divine hints sent to your heart. Pay close attention to every thought that seems to "arrive from nowhere."

3. Ask yourself questions — and wait for the answers

"What's the right decision?" "Is this desire confirmed by God?" — turn these into heartfelt inquiries. Wait for what your soul answers.

4. Test your thoughts

If an idea brings peace and tranquility, it's likely the inner voice. If it stirs anxiety and confusion, it may be the whisper of the ego.

The Child-Seeking Heart: Waiting and the Miracle

Contemplation Questions:

1. Have I ever clearly heard my inner voice in life? Was it right?

2. What dreams have I unconsciously abandoned — without realizing it?

3. Do I treat my heart's desires as "impossible," or do I see them as my divine path?

4. Am I fighting for a child with my mind, but harboring hidden fears in my heart?

The inner voice is God speaking.

To hear it, retreat into stillness. Pray. Purify your heart.

Because children do not come only to the body — they come to the soul.

And the soul can only be reached through the heart.

Rule Seven: The Door of Charity and Generosity

In this journey, one by one, I began to open the locked doors of infertility — with the permission and will of the Creator. Each door, each lock, carried a lesson, a test. They were divine signs placed to remove doubts from my heart and to strengthen my faith. And the final lock was the door of charity and giving. This trial demanded heart, decisiveness, and unwavering determination.

In 2019, my husband and I bought a new house on the outskirts of the city. Since it was purchased on credit, we continued making payments until February 2021. When we finally paid off the debt and felt a sense of lightness in our hearts, the sacred month of Rajab arrived. At that moment, I decided to host a khatm — not merely a tradition, but a heartfelt expression of gratitude and intention.

My decision to hold a khatm was criticized by both my husband and mother-in-law. "Don't waste money on such things," they said. But the peace in my heart and my trust in Allah gave me strength. We invited an imam, and Surah Baqarah was recited. The home was filled with the sound of the Qur'an. It felt as though a divine light shone upon all the pain, doubt, and misconceptions that had accumulated over the years.

Two days after the khatm, I saw a dream in which my late uncle Muhammad visited our home as a guest. Some interpreted this as a sign of glad tidings about a child. But I didn't pay much attention. At the time, my relationship with my husband had become strained — we were on the brink of divorce. There was pressure from many sides. Our parents urged us to separate, and my mother-in-law was already looking for a new bride for her son.

Amid these trying times, I suggested to my husband that we try IVF. We knew it would be a heavy burden — not only emotionally and physically, but financially as well. At the time, this treatment was not available in Uzbekistan. Going to Turkey would cost around $5,000–6,000 — a fantastic sum for us.

Then, one day, I came across an announcement: a Turkish clinic was opening in our own city — Bukhara! Yes, Bukhara — the city where I lived! This wasn't a coincidence; it was a tender sign from destiny itself. The time had come, the heart was ready, the gate of opportunity had opened. The words "ten years, IVF" that had flashed through my heart a decade earlier were now manifesting.

With clear intention and the help of kind acquaintances, I collected $3,000 in loans. My husband hesitated, expressing concerns: "What if it doesn't work?" But I had already surrendered to destiny. One way or another, the path had become clear: either it would happen, or it wouldn't — and I would finally close that chapter in my heart and begin a new one. No more waiting. No more torment.

The treatment began. I was calm. Most importantly, for the first time, I was opening the gate of fate with my own hands. There was a smile on my face and an unquenchable hope in my heart. The doctors' expertise, their compassionate words, their confident eyes — all turned this experience into a spiritual pilgrimage.

And then — about two months later — by the mercy of Allah, I received the most beautiful news of my life: I was pregnant! Of the three women who had undergone IVF treatment that day, I was the only one to receive a positive result.

This was not a personal victory — it was the fruit of sincere faith, the blessing of surrender to divine decree, the miracle granted to a heart that had endured, struggled, and believed. Alhamdulillah!

It was the boundless grace of Allah, His gentle care for me, the sweetest fruit of my long years of patience. I was pregnant with twins — a boy and a girl. We named our son Muhammadjon, after the beloved Prophet Muhammad (peace and blessings be upon him). My husband decided to name our daughter after his grandmother: Saodatkhon.

I am endlessly grateful to the Creator for every single trial I endured. I can never offer enough praise for the countless blessings He has bestowed upon me.

Reflection Questions

1. Has there ever been a test in your life that felt like the final locked door? How did you find the key to open it?

2. Have you ever followed your heart in a situation where everyone else was against it?

3. Have you experienced acting with effort while entrusting the outcome to Allah?

4. Do you believe in divine signs? In what moments of your life have they appeared?

5. If you are standing before a door of trial — where would you begin to open it?

Epilogue

Dear reader, I have shared with you every step I took, every method I tried. I encourage you to try them too. If you find yourself broken by hopelessness, may this book serve as your guiding star, your beacon of light.

Most importantly — never let your hope die. The Almighty, the Creator of all worlds, is never powerless to bless you with children. Believe — truly believe — and your belief will come to life.

Even the fact that you are finishing this book now holds wisdom in itself. It means that if you keep seeking, the locked doors will open one by one — and you will reach the dream you long for, in shaa Allah. Ameen.

Reflection Questions

1. What did I learn from this chapter?
2. What thoughts or emotions did it stir in me?
3. How can I apply this to my daily life?
4. What will I ask from God after reading this?
5. Am I ready to take one small action based on what I read?

Your Notes:

_____

_____

_____

 **Reflection Questions**

1. What did I learn from this chapter?
2. What thoughts or emotions did it stir in me?
3. How can I apply this to my daily life?
4. What will I ask from God after reading this?
5. Am I ready to take one small action based on what I read?

✎ *Your Notes:*

_____

_____

_____

🧠 **Reflection Questions**

1. What did I learn from this chapter?
2. What thoughts or emotions did it stir in me?
3. How can I apply this to my daily life?
4. What will I ask from God after reading this?
5. Am I ready to take one small action based on what I read?

✎ *Your Notes:*

_____

_____

_____

 ## **Reflection Questions**

1. What did I learn from this chapter?
2. What thoughts or emotions did it stir in me?
3. How can I apply this to my daily life?
4. What will I ask from God after reading this?
5. Am I ready to take one small action based on what I read?

 Your Notes:

_____

_____

_____

 ## **Reflection Questions**

1. What did I learn from this chapter?
2. What thoughts or emotions did it stir in me?
3. How can I apply this to my daily life?
4. What will I ask from God after reading this?
5. Am I ready to take one small action based on what I read?

🖊 *Your Notes:*

_____

_____

_____

💭 **Reflection Questions**

1. What did I learn from this chapter?
2. What thoughts or emotions did it stir in me?
3. How can I apply this to my daily life?
4. What will I ask from God after reading this?
5. Am I ready to take one small action based on what I read?

🖊 *Your Notes:*

_____

_____

_____

 **Reflection Questions**

1. What did I learn from this chapter?
2. What thoughts or emotions did it stir in me?
3. How can I apply this to my daily life?
4. What will I ask from God after reading this?
5. Am I ready to take one small action based on what I read?

Your Notes:

_____

_____

_____

About the Author

Dildora Ibrohimova

Dildora Ibrohimova is a journalist and author from Bukhara, Uzbekistan. She currently works as a special correspondent for "Ishonch" ("Trust"), the largest newspaper in Uzbekistan, covering the Bukhara region. Her passion for telling authentic human stories and sincere approach inspired her to write The Child-Seeking Heart: Waiting and the Miracle. Drawing from her personal challenges and victories, this book aims to bring hope and comfort to those experiencing infertility and emotional struggles. Her writing style combines heartfelt honesty with spiritual insight, creating a strong connection with readers. Additionally, Dildora actively participates in community projects that support mental health and family well-being. Through her work, she advocates for compassion and resilience.

www.ingramcontent.com/pod-product-compliance
Lightning Source LLC
LaVergne TN
LVHW041638070526
838199LV00052B/3440